A Note to Parents

DK READERS is a compelling program for beginning readers, designed in conjunction with leading literacy experts, including Dr. Linda Gambrell, Distinguished Professor of Education at Clemson University. Dr. Gambrell has served as President of the National Reading Conference, the College Reading Association, and the International Reading Association.

Beautiful illustrations and superb full-color photographs combine with engaging, easy-to-read stories to offer a fresh approach to each subject in the series. Each DK READER is guaranteed to capture a child's interest while developing his or her reading skills, general knowledge, and love of reading.

The five levels of DK READERS are aimed at different reading abilities, enabling you to choose the books that are exactly right for your child:

Pre-level 1: Learning to read
Level 1: Beginning to read
Level 2: Beginning to read alone
Level 3: Reading alone
Level 4: Proficient readers

The "normal" age at which a child begins to read can be anywhere from three to eight years old. Adult participation through the lower levels is very helpful for providing encouragement, discussing storylines, and sounding out unfamiliar words.

No matter which level you select, you can be sure that you are helping your child learn to read, then read to learn!

DK

LONDON, NEW YORK, MUNICH,
MELBOURNE, AND DELHI

Editor Emma Grange
Designers Jon Hall, Sandra Perry
Senior Pre-Production Producer Jennifer Murray
Producer Louise Minihane
Managing Editor Elizabeth Dowsett
Design Manager Ron Stobbart
Publishing Manager Julie Ferris
Art Director Lisa Lanzarini
Publishing Director Simon Beecroft

Reading Consultant
Linda B. Gambrell, Ph.D.

Dorling Kindersley would like to thank: Randi Sørensen and
Robert Stefan Ekblom at the LEGO Group and J. W. Rinzler,
Leland Chee, Troy Alders, and Carol Roeder at Lucasfilm.

First American Edition, 2014
10 9 8 7 6 5 4 3 2 1
Published in the United States by DK Publishing
4th Floor, 345 Hudson Street, New York, New York 10014

001–196542–July/14

DK books are available at special discounts when purchased in bulk
for sales promotions, premiums, fund-raising, or educational use.
For details, contact: DK Publishing Special Markets, 4th Floor,
345 Hudson Street, New York, New York 10014
SpecialSales@dk.com

A catalog record for this book is available
from the Library of Congress.

ISBN: 978-1-4654-2029-9 (Paperback)
ISBN: 978-1-4654-2028-2 (Hardcover)

Color reproduction in the UK by Altaimage
Printed and bound in China

All other images © Dorling Kindersley
For further information see: www.dkimages.com

Discover more at
www.dk.com
www.starwars.com
www.LEGO.com/starwars

Contents

DK

BEGINNING
2
TO READ ALONE

LEGO STAR WARS

THE EMPIRE STRIKES BACK™

Written by
Emma Grange

An evil Empire

The Emperor is angry.

He has taken over the galaxy,
but some rebels are trying
to stop him.

Darth Vader   Darth Sidious

The Emperor is an evil Sith
Lord named Darth Sidious. He has
an apprentice named Darth Vader.

Darth Sidious tells Darth
Vader that the rebels must
be found and destroyed.

Darth Vader obeys his Master.
He sends probe droids to search
the galaxy for the rebels.

The Sith
The evil Sith seek power
for themselves. There are
only two Sith at one time:
a Master and an apprentice.

The rebels

Here are the rebels.
They are hiding in a far
corner of the galaxy on
a planet called Hoth.

Hoth

Han Solo   Luke Skywalker   Princess Leia

Luke Skywalker is a very special rebel. His father was once a famous Jedi. Now Luke wants to become a Jedi, too.

Luke has many friends among the rebels. They are all prepared to fight the Empire.

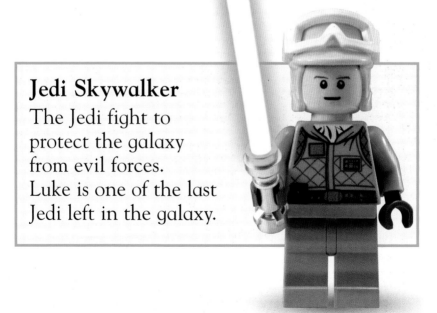

Jedi Skywalker
The Jedi fight to protect the galaxy from evil forces. Luke is one of the last Jedi left in the galaxy.

Rebel base

The galaxy is full of many kinds of planets. Hoth is a cold place, covered in snow and ice. Nobody lives here, which makes it an excellent place to hide.

The rebels have built a secret base. Here it is, hidden in the snow.

The rebels are planning an attack on the Empire.

They need to hurry, because Darth Vader's probe droids are on their way!

Probe Droid

Probe droids are programmed to search for people and objects without being spotted.

Chewbacca

Princess Leia

Wampa attack

There are dangerous creatures lurking in Hoth's snowdrifts. This hairy beast with sharp claws and horns is a wampa.

It has captured Luke and taken him back to its cave. Wampas are carnivores and like to eat people. Look out, Luke!

Luckily, Han
Solo notices that
Luke is missing and
rushes to rescue him.

Bacta Tank
After freezing in the cold,
Luke undergoes medical
treatment in a bacta
tank. The tank contains
special healing liquid.

The Battle of Hoth

Nothing stays a secret from the Empire for long. Darth Vader's probe droids have discovered the rebels on Hoth.

The Sith Lord sends an army to Hoth to destroy the base.

Giant AT-AT walkers march across the snow, firing at the rebels. They trample anything that gets in their way.

Snowspeeder

Rebel pilots try to bring down the AT-ATs with their agile snowspeeders, but the enemy vehicles are too powerful.

AT-AT walker

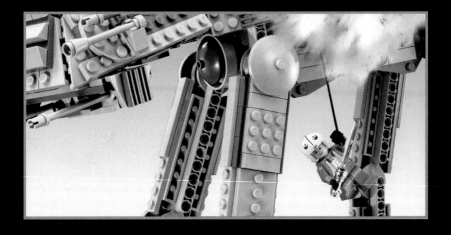

Brave rebels

Luke has a cunning plan.
He climbs up one of the AT-ATs
and destroys it from the inside!

Millennium
Falcon

The rebels fight the Empire's army bravely, but they are not able to stop the Empire from blowing up their base on Hoth.

Just in time, Han Solo escapes with Princess Leia in his ship, the *Millennium Falcon*, while Luke zooms off in his X-wing. Where will they go now?

X-wing

Jedi training

Who is this green creature?

On the dark and swampy planet of Dagobah, Luke has found Yoda, the greatest Jedi Master of all time. Now Luke can begin his Jedi training.

Yoda may be small and old, but he is wise and strong. He teaches Luke to control the Force and resist the dark side.

The Sith use the dark side of the Force for evil, but the Jedi believe in using their powers only for good.

The Force
The Force is a powerful energy used by the Jedi and the Sith. Yoda uses it to lift Luke's X-wing out of the swamp!

Bounty hunters

Darth Vader is determined
to capture Luke Skywalker.
He knows that the young Jedi is
powerful and wants him stopped.

Dengar

IG-88

These suspicious looking criminals are bounty hunters.

Bounty hunters will work for anyone who will pay them a high price. They specialize in hunting down and capturing people. Darth Vader wants them to capture Luke and his friends!

Boba Fett

Bossk

Boba Fett

This bounty hunter is
Boba Fett. He has been
promised a large reward
if he captures Han Solo.

rangefinder

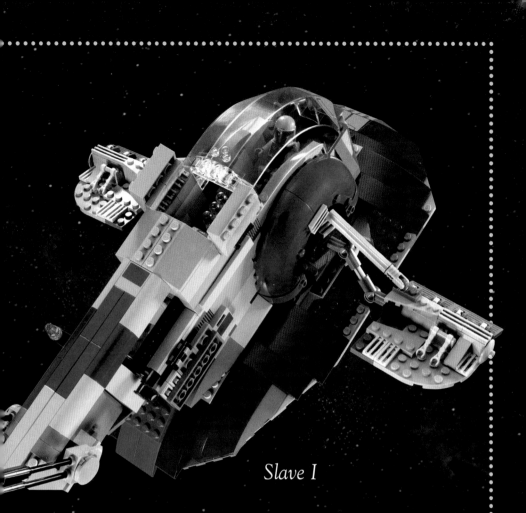

Slave I

Boba Fett has a ship called *Slave I*. He uses his tracking skills to follow Han Solo's *Millennium Falcon.*

Cloud City

Han Solo and Princess Leia flee to Cloud City. This city floats high among the clouds, and is ruled by Lando Calrissian, an old friend of Han's.

Lando Calrissian

Lando used to be a smuggler. Can he be trusted to help Han?

Lando doesn't tell Han that Boba Fett followed them all the way to Cloud City. Darth Vader is now waiting for them. Uh-oh!

Trapped!
Darth Vader's fierce stormtroopers surround the rebels. It looks like there is no way out!

Shocking truth

Through the power of the Force, Luke senses that his friends are in trouble. But he arrives too late—and comes face to face with Darth Vader!

Luke puts his new Jedi skills to the test as he duels the evil Sith Lord.

Darth Vader tries to convince
Luke to join the dark side.
Finally, he reveals the truth:
Darth Vader is Luke's father!

Friends to the rescue

What will happen to the rebels next? Han Solo has been captured by Boba Fett. Despite fighting bravely, Luke has been injured by Darth Vader.

Lando Calrissian is sorry that he couldn't stop Han from being captured. He manages to escape Cloud City with Princess Leia. As they leave, they also manage to rescue Luke.

Dark times

As Darth Vader returns to the Emperor, it looks like the Empire is stronger than ever.

The rebels have suffered several defeats.

Some of them, like Han Solo, have been captured, but his loyal friends are flying off to rescue him.

The rebels won't give up hope just yet!

Quiz

1. What planet were the rebels hiding on?

2. What type of droid is this?

3. What is this person's job?

4. What is Boba Fett's ship called?

5. Who does Luke Skywalker find on the planet Dagobah?

1. Hoth 2. Probe droid 3. Bounty hunter 4. *Slave 1* 5. Yoda

Index

Here are some other DK Readers you might enjoy.

Level 2

LEGO® *Star Wars*® The Phantom Menace™
Who has brought the LEGO® *Star Wars*® galaxy
to the brink of war? Can the Jedi stop them?

LEGO® *Star Wars*® Attack of the Clones™
Meet evil Count Dooku! Can the Republic's
clone troopers defeat the Sith's droid army?

Angry Birds™ *Star Wars*® Path to the Pork Side
Can Redkin Skywalker resist the power of the
Pork Side? Join the young Jedi Bird on his journey!

Level 3

LEGO® *Star Wars*® Revenge of the Sith™
The Jedi must save the galaxy from the Sith!
Will Anakin fall to the dark side?

LEGO® *Star Wars*® Return of the Jedi™
Luke Skywalker is the last Jedi in the galaxy.
Can he help the rebels defeat the evil Empire?

LEGO® Legends of Chima™: Race for CHI
Jump into battle with the animal tribes as
they fight to get their claws on the CHI!